450 SIGHT WORDS

TRACING WITH PHONICS

Handwriting
practice for kids,
letter tracing,
reading, spellings and phonics

For Kindergarten, Grade 1 & 2

BELLYBEES BOOKS

Copyright © 2023 by Bellybees Incorporated All rights reserved. No part of this publication may be reproduced, stored or transmitted in any form or by any means, electronic, mechanical, photocopying, recording, scanning, or otherwise without written permission from the publisher. It is illegal to copy this book, post it to a website, or distribute it by any other means without permission.

@bellybeesproducts
www.bellybees.com

450 SIGHT WORDS

TRACING WITH PHONICS

Handwriting
practice for kids,
letter tracing,
reading, spellings and phonics

For Kindergarten, Grade 1 & 2

BELLYBEES BOOKS

Word Trace

Alphabet A - Z

Aa Aa

Bb Bb

Cc Cc

Dd Dd

Ee Ee

Ff Ff

Gg Gg

Hh Hh

Ii Ii

Alphabet A - Z

Jj Jj

Kk Kk

Ll Ll

Mm Mm

Nn Nn

Oo Oo

Pp Pp

Qq Qq

Rr Rr

Alphabet A - Z

Ss Ss

Tt Tt

Uu Uu

Vv Vv

Ww Ww

Xx Xx

Yy Yy

Zz Zz

Trace words that begin with the letter

Aa

ant

anchor

astronaut

apple

alligator

airplane

Trace words that begin with the letter

Bb

bee

baby

ball

book

bat

button

Trace words that begin with the letter

Cc

cookie

cat

cloud

clown

cup

cow

Trace words that begin with the letter

Dd

doughnut

dinosaur

doctor

door

dog

dad

Trace words that begin with the letter

Ee

elephant

earth

egg

eagle

envelope

ear

Trace words that begin with the letter

Ff

fish

flower

finger

fire

food

frog

Trace words that begin with the letter

Gg

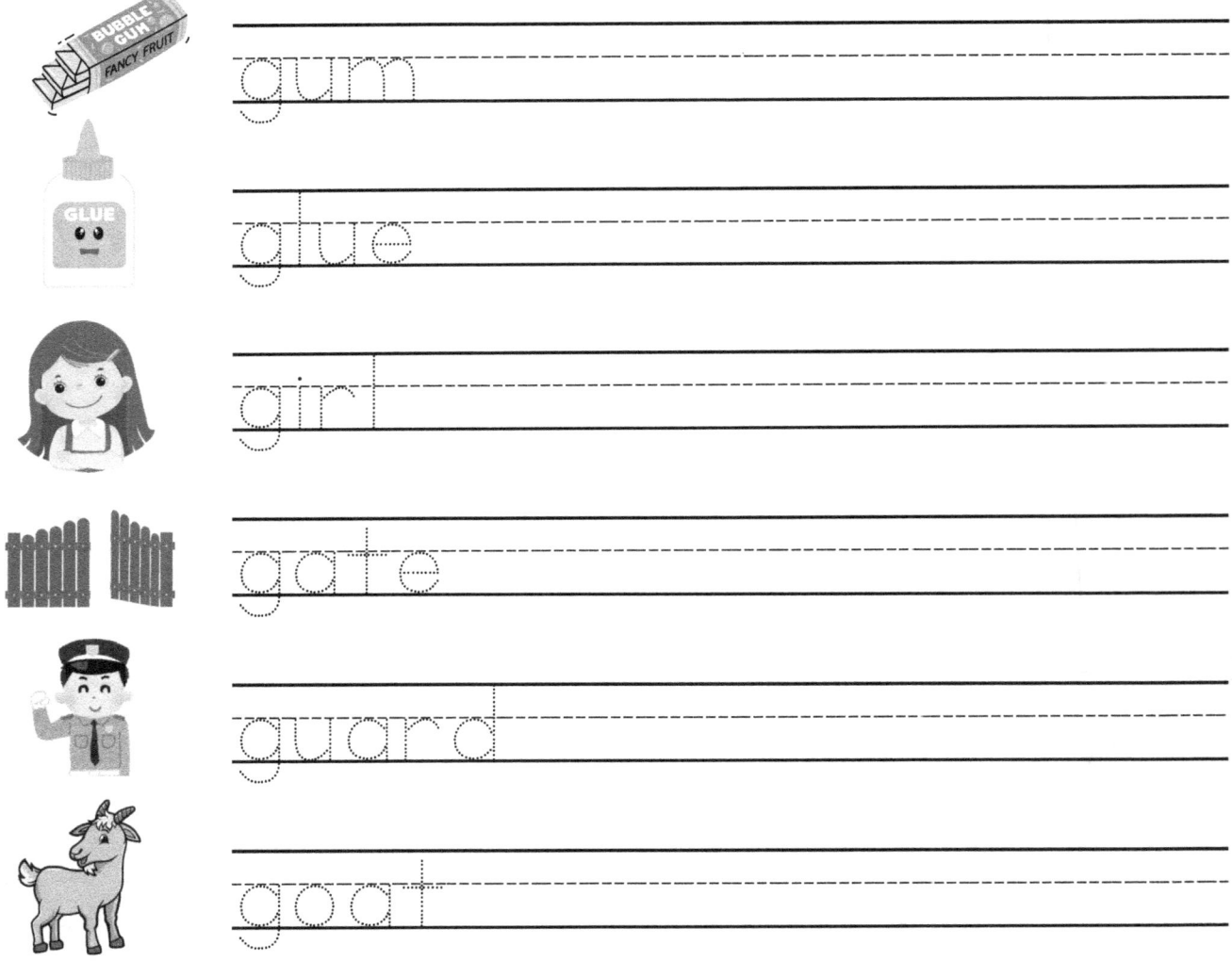

gum

glue

girl

gate

guard

goat

Trace words that begin with the letter

Hh

horse

house

hammock

hat

heart

hand

Trace words that begin with the letter

Ii

ice cream

igloo

island

ink

ice

iron

Trace words that begin with the letter

Jj

jug

jeep

juice

jacket

jam

jellyfish

Trace words that begin with the letter

Kk

kangaroo

kite

key

ketchup

kettle

koala

Trace words that begin with the letter

Ll

leaf

lemon

lion

letter

lamp

lock

Trace words that begin with the letter

Mm

monkey

map

moon

milk

money

mango

Trace words that begin with the letter

Nn

nut

nose

noodle

nurse

nest

needle

Trace words that begin with the letter

Oo

orange

onion

otter

oven

octopus

oval

Trace words that begin with the letter

Pp

pumpkin

pineapple

pen

puppy

pizza

pig

Trace words that begin with the letter

Qq

quilt

question

quail

queen

quarter

quiver

Trace words that begin with the letter

Rr

rabbit

rainbow

rose

river

ribbon

run

Trace words that begin with the letter

Ss

Trace words that begin with the letter

Tt

train

tiger

tent

turtle

tomato

tree

Trace words that begin with the letter

Uu

umbrella

urn

uniform

unicorn

uranus

up

Trace words that begin with the letter

Vv

Trace words that begin with the letter

Ww

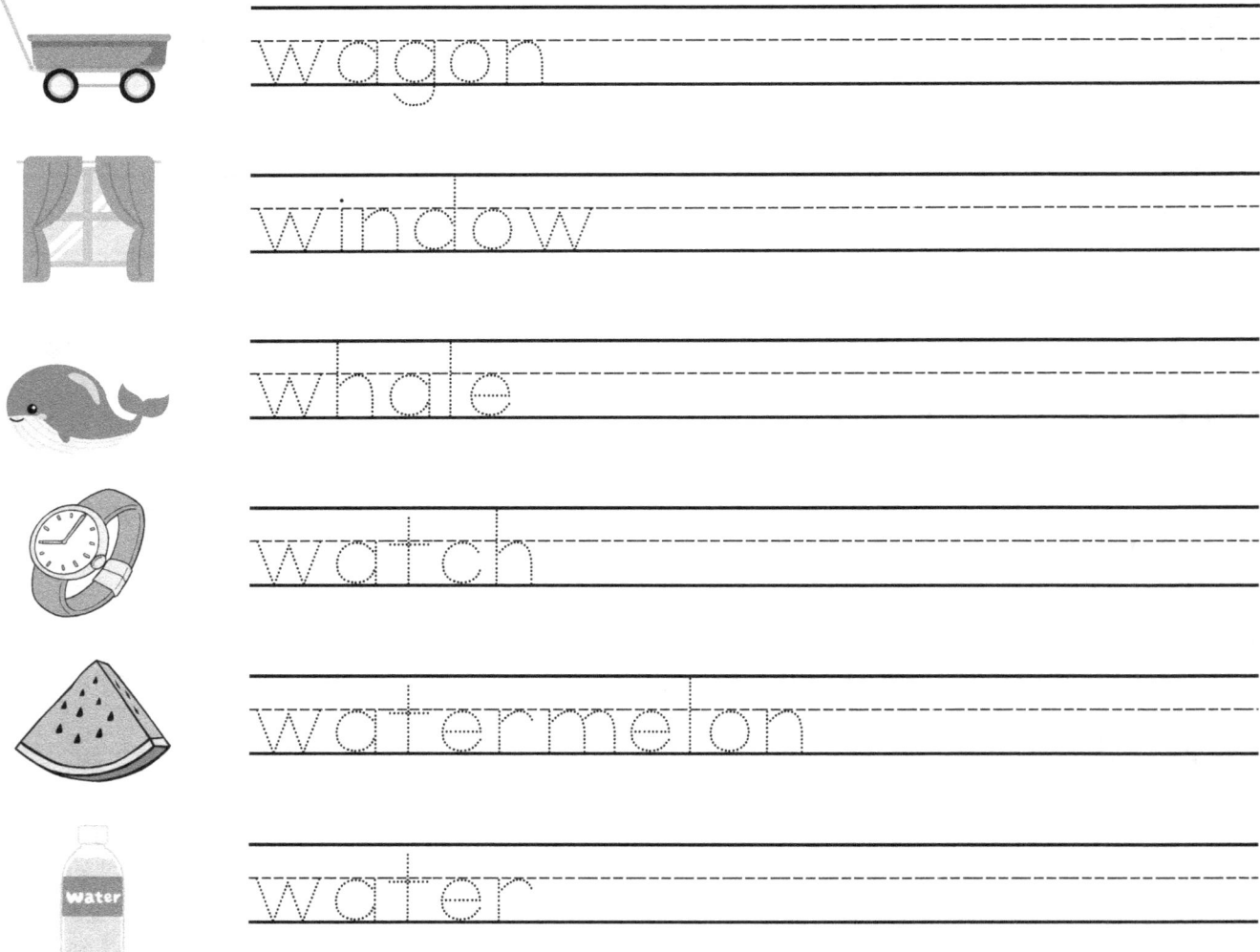

wagon

window

whale

watch

watermelon

water

Trace words that begin with the letter

Xx

x-ray

x-mas

xylophone

xerox

ximenia

xerus

Trace words that begin with the letter

Yy

yo-yo

yak

yacht

yogurt

yarn

yoga

Trace words that begin with the letter

Zz

zebra

zoo

zipper

zucchini

zero

zigzag

Trace words that include

at

bat

cat

hat

mat

chat

rat

Trace words that include

ate

date

fate

slate

mate

crate

plate

Trace words that include

an

and

can

man

sand

plan

land

Trace words that include

ane

cane

lane

mane

pane

crane

plane

Trace words that include

ain

gain

main

pain

rain

main

train

Trace words that include

ap

cap

gap

tap

map

nap

strap

Trace words that include

ape

cape

gape

nape

tape

drape

shape

Trace words that include

en

den

hen

send

ten

then

friend

Trace words that include

ee

sleep

keep

green

feet

sweep

weep

Trace words that include

et

get

bet

met

wet

yet

set

Trace words that include

ed

bed

fed

red

led

petted

shed

Trace words that include

ell

fell

yell

bell

sell

tell

shell

Trace words that include

ight

night

sight

might

bright

flight

eight

Trace words that include

old

cold

sold

fold

told

bold

mold

Trace words that include

OW

cow

how

owl

bow

chow

towel

Trace words that include

ea

eat

seat

meat

bean

lean

team

Trace words that include

ut

but

cut

shut

butter

mut

rut

Trace words that include

ute

cute

flute

lute

mute

brute

jute

Trace words that include

ot

got

hot

pot

lot

not

shot

Trace words that include

oa

goat

road

board

toad

coat

goat

Trace words that include

foot

moon

spoon

door

wood

food

Trace words that include

in

bin

win

sing

wind

mind

chin

Trace words that include

ine

mine

spine

shine

nine

pine

fine

Trace words that include

bit

pit

hit

sit

spit

fit

Trace words that include

ite

bite

site

might

write

quite

kite

Trace words that include

er

singer

finger

fern

perm

stern

perk

Trace words that include

est

best

nest

pest

test

smallest

bravest

Trace words that include

ar

car

star

park

cart

start

dark

Trace words that include

ore

bore

more

pore

tore

sore

chore

Trace words that include

ur

blur

hurt

turn

fur

burst

hurt

Trace words that include

ay

say

pay

tay

day

pray

bay

Trace words that include

un

sun

fun

bun

until

under

untie

Trace words that include

all

ball

call

mall

tall

fall

stall

Trace words that include

ou

found

proud

mound

around

pound

hound

Trace basic sight words

I

the

a

he

she

me

we

be

Trace basic sight words

is

was

to

do

are

all

as

has

Trace basic sight words

you

your

come

some

came

said

here

there

Trace basic sight words

they

him

go

no

so

my

one

by

Trace basic sight words

only

old

like

have

of

live

give

day

Trace basic sight words

play

away

for

how

now

into

back

little

Trace basic sight words

down

what

when

why

where

who

which

don't

Trace basic sight words

asked

this

any

many

more

before

were

our

Trace basic sight words

because

want

saw

put

going

us

mother

father

Trace basic sight words

sister

brother

very

could

should

would

will

over

Trace basic sight words

right

too

two

four

goes

does

made

their

www.ingramcontent.com/pod-product-compliance
Lightning Source LLC
Chambersburg PA
CBHW082212070526
44585CB00020B/2378